AWAKEN
— THE —
INNER
ALCHEMIST

33 PRINCIPLES TO TRANSFORM
PAIN INTO POWER AND
LIVE WITH PURPOSE

FREDERICK A. MARTINEZ

Printed in the United States of America.
Book design by (Frederick A. Martinez)
Cover design by (Frederick A. Martinez)

ISBN – eBook: 978-1-965761-52-6
ISBN – Paperback: 978-1-965761-53-3
ISBN – Ingram Spark: 978-1-965761-54-0
Library of Congress Control Number: 2025914451
First Edition: August 2025

Connect with Fred:
www.FredMartinez.info

AWAKEN

— THE —

INNER

ALCHEMIST

33 PRINCIPLES TO TRANSFORM
PAIN INTO POWER AND
LIVE WITH PURPOSE

FREDERICK A. MARTINEZ

SPOTLIGHT
PUBLISHING HOUSE
Goodyear, AZ

TABLE OF CONTENTS

WHAT DOES INNER ALCHEMIST MEAN TO YOU?

Everyone has their own take on it. And that's the beauty of it. To me, an Inner Alchemist chooses to turn their deepest challenges into their most powerful strengths. It's the part of you that doesn't just cope with pain—it thrives from it. It doesn't just survive—it flourishes. It's the quiet, yet powerful force within you that knows:

- Don't see your wounds as weaknesses; think of them as building blocks.
- Don't let your fears hold you back; instead, see them as a cue to dig deeper.
- Don't let your past hold you back – it's an opportunity to shape your future.

Awakening the Inner Alchemist is about reclaiming control of your life and becoming the writer of your own story. It's the moment you stop fleeing from your past and start rewriting it with truth, love, purpose, and strength. This isn't just a spiritual journey – it's intensely personal and practical. You take what others use as excuses and turn them into chances. You confront the darkness directly, armed with light. You stop asking "Why me?" and start saying "Watch me." Alchemy isn't about turning base metals into gold – it's about aligning yourself with your true self. It's about transforming inner turmoil into peace, using your triggers as guides, and turning resistance into resilience. That's where the real value lies.

Don't mistake this book for a motivational guide – it's about transformation. It's not about reinventing yourself, but rather about reconnecting with the person you were before society told you who you should be. That's what the Inner Alchemist is all about: the 33 Principles of transformation.

WHY 33 PRINCIPLES?

You might be asking: why 33? It's because 33 is more than just a number – it's a framework. Your spine has 33 vertebrae, which keep you standing tall. They help you stand, move around, and carry your weight, just like these principles. Each one acts like a vertebra, a support system. They reinforce your spiritual, emotional, mental, and physical alignment.

Jesus was 33 years old when he finished his mission on earth. Whether you view it as a historical fact or a symbolic representation, the message remains the same: 33 signifies sacred completion, transcending struggle, and stepping into purpose.

In numerology, 33 is known as the Master Teacher. It represents the trinity—mind, body, and spirit—multiplied by divine wisdom.

Three is the number of wholeness:

1. Past, present, future;
2. Father, Son, Holy Spirit;
3. Thought, word, action.

Eleven represents spiritual insight. Here are the specific spiritual insights:

1. **You are not your past.**
   Your story has made you who you are, but it's not who you are. Your identity isn't found in your pain—it's in how you transform it.

2. **Your soul knows the way.**
   Logic has its limits, but intuition is your inner guide. Trust the quiet voice inside you over the loud distractions around you.

3. **Energy never lies.**
   Words can be deceiving. Appearances can be misleading. But energy? It speaks the truth. Pay attention to how people and situations feel, not just how they seem.

4. **The universe responds to alignment, not effort.**
   Running on scarcity leaves you exhausted. Operating from a place of truth gives you power. You don't attract what you want—you attract who you are.

5. **Everything is happening *for* you, not *to* you.**
   Even the pain, especially the pain. Every breakdown is a step forward, a breadcrumb that guides you toward a breakthrough.

6. **Presence is power.**
   Regret dwells in the past. Anxiety is tied to the future. Freedom resides in the present moment. Keep your feet on the ground. Take one breath at a time.

7. **You are the observer, not the emotion.**
   Emotions are just energy flowing through you. You don't need to cling to them. You can witness, listen, and let them go.

8. **Letting go is not weakness—it's wisdom.**
   Detachment isn't about being apathetic. It's about having the courage to let go of what's not yours to control.

9. **Forgiveness frees *you*.**
   It's not about excusing behavior. It's about letting go of the poison holding you back from moving forward.

10. **Self-love is a spiritual practice.**
    It's not about ego or arrogance. It's about believing, "I am enough. I am worthy. I am sacred," and living that truth.

11. **You are a vessel for something bigger.**
    Nothing about you is by chance. Your gifts and voice are all meant to uplift, awaken, and bring light to the world.

By multiplying the two, you arrive at 33—a cosmic reminder that your life is not random, but divinely planned. These aren't just 33 lessons to recall; they're 33 invitations to embody, to live with intention, and to lead by being your authentic self. You're not here to follow someone else's path but tap into your divine purpose.

The world doesn't need more people seeking validation; it needs people living in alignment, rooted in truth, and leading with their hearts. That's what these 33 principles are meant to do. They don't guide you through life; they guide you back to your true self.

Let's get started.

Principle 1

Live and Lead With Integrity

*"Our ability to handle life's challenges
is a measure of our strength of character."*
~ Les Brown

"Integrity isn't tested when everyone is watching—it's tested when no one is."

What does it mean to live with integrity?

Does it mean always doing the right thing, no matter who's watching?

That's part of it, but it's more than that.

Living with integrity means having your inner and outer worlds in sync. You speak your mind, keep your promises, and follow through on your commitments—even when it's tough, expensive, or no one else is doing it.

It's easy to live with integrity when others are watching. It's easy when people applaud, praise, or put you in the spotlight. But absolute integrity is built in the dark, when you're alone with your choices, values, and conscience.

It's the moment when you could take the easy route, but you don't. It's when you're tempted to lie, but you decide to tell the truth. You honor your commitments not because they are written down but because they are who you are.

Do you hold yourself to the same standard when there's no one to impress, no prize to win, and no audience to perform for?

Start with trust. Start with peace. Build your life on integrity that stays the same, no matter who's around.

One Man's Act of Kindness

A man noticed someone drop their wallet in a crowded train station. He picked it up without anyone noticing and with no cameras around. When he opened it, he found cash, credit cards, and even a winning lottery ticket.

His mind began to spin:

"No one would ever know..."
"This could change everything..."
"Maybe this is a sign from the universe."

But then he caught himself. He took a deep breath and reminded himself of something straightforward: "Integrity isn't tested when everyone is watching, it's tested when no one is."

He tracked down the guy, returned the wallet, and kept moving. There was no fanfare, no social media post—just a simple act of kindness.

Later, someone who saw it said, "You're a good man." He shrugged and replied, "I'm just a guy who knows who he is."

That's what strength of character looks like—quiet, steady, and real. It's not about being perfect. It's about aligning with who you are and how you show up, even when no one else would know the difference.

Relentless Integrity: The Trusted Tool

Relentless integrity is like the one tool you can always rely on in your toolbox—the one that's old, scratched, and worn but always gets the job done.

That's what relentless integrity is like in a person. You might not be the flashiest, but people know they can count on you when it counts. You don't take shortcuts. You don't shift your values when it's convenient. You don't compromise when pressure rises.

You don't need to explain yourself when you're built on integrity. You show up. Consistently. Quietly. Fully.

Integrity isn't about being honest when it's easy. It's about standing firm when no one's watching, when there's a benefit to cutting corners, when everyone else is lowering their standards.

You do the right thing not because it'll be noticed, but because it's who you are.

Six Anchors for Relentless Integrity

1. **Know your values—or you'll fall for anything.**
   Document them. Guard them. Revisit them. Without clarity, life will pull you in every direction.

2. **Say what you mean. Mean what you say.**
   Don't sugarcoat, overpromise, or exaggerate. Let your word be enough.

3. **Make decisions that let you sleep at night.**
   Not "Did I win?" but "Did I stay true?"

4. **Own your mistakes—fast.**
   Don't deflect. Don't delay. Take responsibility. Learn. Move forward.

5. **Keep your circle honest.**
   Surround yourself with people who sharpen you, not flatter you. Real ones challenge your blind spots.

6. **Practice when it's small so you're ready when it's big.**
   Integrity in the little things builds the muscle for the big ones. How you act when no one's watching shapes who you are when everyone is.

An Inner Alchemist doesn't just speak truth—they live it. Not for applause. Not for appearance. But for alignment. Because the peace that comes from living with integrity is more valuable than any external reward.

Thought-Provoking Question

Where do your actions fall short of your values in life, and what would it take to bring yourself back into alignment?

PRINCIPLE 2

MASTER YOUR EMOTIONS

"What happens is not as important
as how you react to what happens."
~ Ellen Glasgow

Today's world rewards hard work and quick thinking. But what about emotional control? That's the hidden skill most people never master, and it's the one that keeps your life steady amid chaos.

Life can be pretty chaotic, honestly. You're bound to run into unexpected situations. People will cut you off in traffic, ignore you, lie, let you down, or combine all these things. That's just how life goes. But how you respond is entirely up to you.

Many people react impulsively, letting their emotions take over their day. However, by learning to manage your emotions, you can develop the ability to **STOP**, **THINK**, and **ACT**—not driven by ego, but by awareness.

Emotions are like clouds in the sky—they come and go. But if you grasp onto them, hold on tight; if you keep dwelling on the story, they become heavier. It's like filling up a backpack with weights: anger, regret, shame, jealousy—one by one. At first, it doesn't seem like much. But over time, you're trudging through life feeling drained, wondering why everything feels so burdensome.

Consider it like this: every time you replay an old story or let a negative thought spin out of control, add another brick to your backpack. One brick might not seem like much, but over time, that weight builds up, and now you're trudging through life with emotional baggage, wondering why you're feeling so drained. The truth is, many people are weighed down by things they've never let go of. Not because they can't, but because they never take a moment to examine what they're carrying.

You regain control when you slow down and look at what's in your hands. You acknowledge the feeling, see it for what it is, and start to let it go. As you shed weight, you finally start to breathe freely again.

Learning to manage your emotions is a continuous journey; you don't just seek calm, you cultivate it.

Mastering Your Emotions in 3 Simple Steps

STEP 1: STOP: Pause the spiral. Interrupt the pattern.

- Name what you feel.
  Anger? Shame? Jealousy? Fear? Name it—and you can gain control over it.
- Take 3 deep breaths.
  That pause brings calmness. It gives you control again.
- Walk it off. Move your body.
  Emotions get stuck, but motion can shake them free.

STEP 2: THINK: Don't let the feeling hijack the meaning.

- Ask yourself:
  "Is this thought helpful?"
  "Is it even true?"
  If not, try rephrasing it. You're not pushing away your emotions; you're reclaiming your power.

6

- Use the 90-Second Rule.
  Let the wave roll through. Then figure out how you want to catch it.

STEP 3: ACT: Respond with intention, not reaction.

- Write it down. Let the page take the weight that your chest doesn't need to carry.
- Fuel your body. Take care of your body by eating clean, staying hydrated, and getting enough sleep. Your physical health has a direct impact on your emotional well-being.
- Choose your people. Be around people who bring you down to earth, not those who drain your energy.
- Give yourself grace. Mastering something isn't about being perfect. It's about bouncing back even faster the next time.

Thought-Provoking Question

What would your best self do when emotions start to overwhelm you?

PRINCIPLE 3

VULNERABILITY
IS STRENGTH

"To become different from what we are,
we must have some awareness of what we are."
~ Bruce Lee

For a long time, we were led to believe that vulnerability is a sign of weakness, that being strong means being invulnerable, and that being genuine, showing emotion, or discussing pain makes us less powerful. But that's not the case. By owning your vulnerability, you gain a sense of power.

Bruce Lee wasn't always trying to come across as tough. He knew that flow is more powerful than force, and self-awareness is more powerful than ego. You don't become strong by pretending you're invincible. You become strong by acknowledging your weaknesses and deciding to face them head-on.

Being vulnerable means being honest, without any pretenses. It's a moment when you stop doing and start being. You have to let go of hiding behind your accomplishments, your image, and your defenses and speak the truth.

Connection happens when you're willing to be vulnerable. People don't bond with ideals; they connect with the real person behind them. They relate to the raw, authentic part of you that's willing to be open and honest.

Breaking the Mask: My Journey. For years, I wore a mask, playing the role of the tough one, the one people relied on. I was the athlete, the engineer, the go-getter who always figured it out and got things done. But there was a time when I struggled deeply, both mentally and emotionally, and I didn't want anyone to know. I feared that if I opened up, people would see me differently, maybe even think I was weak or lose respect for me.

But keeping it a secret didn't make me stronger – it made me feel more isolated. Then, one day, I finally cracked. For the first time, I stopped pretending when talking to someone I trusted. I said, "I'm tired." I'm scared. I'm going through things I can't even put into words. And I feel like I should always be tough, but I'm not. And you know what happened? They didn't back away. They came closer.

Back then, I learned that being genuine builds trust faster than being tough. By being true to myself, I created space for others to be open, too. I made room for more than just casual conversation.

Being vulnerable doesn't make you weak; it makes you human. It encourages others to let their guard down. It builds connections and bridges gaps. It brings people closer together, whether in romantic relationships, friendships, teams, or families.

When you say you're struggling, when you share how you got that scar, when you say, "I don't have it all figured out, but I'm working on it," you have a strength that many people are afraid to show. That's what it means to be a leader.

Bruce Lee stated, "Be like water." Water doesn't fight back. It moves. It changes. It changes shape as it touches something and wears down mountains over time through patience and determination.

Weakness is like water. It softens the tough parts of you. It brings the truth to light. And over time, it makes you unbreakable—not because you're tough, but because you're whole.

Thought-Provoking Question

What mask are you ready to let go of, and who could you finally connect with once you do?

PRINCIPLE 4

DISCIPLINE: YOUR INNER FUEL

"Anyone who has never made a mistake
has never tried anything new."
~ Albert Einstein

Let's face it, motivation is like sugar – it gives you a quick rush, but it won't sustain you. It's not the kind of fuel you need to grow and thrive. Some social media influencers talk a good game to get views, but do they actually live it, breathe it, and share it? In my experience, there are three types of experts: those who have walked the walk, those who are still doing it, and those who study it.

Success isn't an instant achievement. It develops through consistent, everyday efforts that build up over time. Discipline is the backbone of it all, even if motivation gives you a spark of inspiration.

It begins with planting the seeds of your desires in life and nurturing them every day, without worrying about whether they're taking root. You need to have faith that the process will unfold. Would you question a tree's roots just because you can't see them?

Today's the time to plant the seeds for your future. The choices you make now will shape who you become in five years:

- The books you read
- The food you eat
- The exercise you do
- The people you spend time with
- Your close relationships
- The videos you watch
- The music you listen to
- The people you follow on social media
- Your daily habits
- The things you say to yourself

These aren't just actions you take. They're seeds that will sprout, whether you realize it or not. So, consider this: Are you planting weeds or building a garden? What can you do today that your future self will thank you for tomorrow?

"To be able to control your impulses and put off getting what you want right away in order to get bigger rewards later on is the most important thing you need to do to be successful."
— Brian Tracy

Don't give up on living a joyful life because you're putting off getting what you want. It's about not sacrificing your future for a little bit of fun.

Yes, focus on the present. But don't forget to lay the groundwork to make the future even brighter.

Every meal, moment, conversation, and workout you have either moves you closer to becoming who you want to be or pushes you further away.

Think about this. Is this moment serving a purpose or just filling space? Am I creating something or just going through the motions?

Discipline isn't about just saying no; it's about setting direction.

Knowledge isn't the issue; it's self-discipline. You already know what to do, but the tough part is following through consistently. Discipline is about choosing long-term benefits over immediate gratification. It's about pushing through fatigue, making healthy choices when you crave junk food, and sticking to your goals even when you don't feel like it.

Discipline is what drives the alchemist's journey. It may not be glamorous, but it's a powerful force. Discipline brings freedom, while motivation is fleeting.

Thought-Provoking Question

What's one thing you can do today that your future self will appreciate tomorrow?

PRINCIPLE 5

LET GO TO GROW

"Some of us think holding on makes us strong;
but sometimes it is letting go."
~ Hermann Hesse

What's holding you back from becoming the person you're meant to be? You can't grow by clinging to the past. You grow by letting go of what's no longer serving you.

Ever tried holding water in a tight fist? You get nothing. It just passes right through. But if you open your hand like a bowl, it's easy to hold that water. That's what it means to let go—to be open to receiving.

Imagine this: You dive your clenched fist into the water. What do you pull up?

Nothing. The water flows away. But now open your hand, palm up like a bowl. What happens? You catch water. You receive it. That's life. That's energy. That's growth.

Nothing can stay when you're anxious, controlling, and clinging to a specific outcome. You're pushing away what you're desperately trying to keep. But when you let go of trying to control things and stop fighting, you make room for what you truly want.

Releasing something doesn't mean you stop caring about it; it means you trust enough to stay open to new possibilities. By letting go, you approach life more thoughtfully and with greater freedom. Letting go is the key to letting nature take its course. According to the Tao, the more we try to push growth, the more we block it from happening. It's like a farmer overwatering a seed - we suffocate its potential when we try to control it too much.

Here are ten essential types of release that pave the way for genuine growth:

1. **The Art of Not Doing**:
    Real power comes from knowing when to act and when to step back. We often try to control everything, but too much control can actually hinder progress.

    Take planting a tree, for example. You provide good soil, water it, and then let it be. If you constantly tug on the roots, it won't grow. The same principle applies to dating. Attraction is like a seed; you plant it by showing interest, but if you text too much or push too hard, you smother it.

    Growth needs space. A farmer doesn't dig up the seed every day to check on its roots. They have faith in the process, and you should too.

2. **Accepting Change**:
    Life is constantly changing. It has its ups and downs, its dark and light moments. When we resist, we become rigid and exhausted from fighting against the current. Let go, and the current will carry you forward. Let go, and life will flow with you. Instead of trying to fix all your flaws, focus on what you do best. That's not weakness,

it's wisdom. You can grow when you release the things that aren't serving you.

3. **Letting go of the outcome**:
   When you worry about the result, you miss out on the present. Worry is all about the future, taking you out of the moment.

   Imagine watching a basketball game without paying attention to the players, just the score. That's what it feels like to focus on results. You miss the beauty of the play. The fun is in the process, not just the outcome.

   Have faith in your preparation, and let go of the outcome. Be present in the moment, and enjoy the ride.

4. **Letting go of what doesn't serve you:**
   Wild animals don't store anything up. They don't worry about status. They only have what they need to survive. That's all there is to it.

   But at some point, we forgot this. We chase comfort in things like perfect haircuts, the right clothes, and the right image. But the truth is, having more doesn't bring serenity. It comes from having enough.

   Letting go doesn't mean giving up. It's about making room. It's about releasing things that hold you back, like old expectations, bad relationships, habits that drain you, and identities that no longer fit.

   My parents taught me that being moderate is being free. That you finally have room for what matters when you stop filling your life with things that don't.

5. **Letting go helps you grow:**
   You lose more when you hold on. Nothing stays when you try to grip water with a closed fist. But let go of your grip and open your hand. That's when life starts to come in.

   Letting go isn't weak; it's smart. It's choosing to be aligned instead of attached. It says, "This doesn't work for me anymore," and believes that what you want will come to you without you having to force it.

6. **Letting go of control:**
   Trying to control everything is like trying to hold the tide with your hands. You might feel powerful for a moment, but eventually, you drown in your own resistance. You can't control outcomes, people, or timing. But you *can* control your:

   • Effort
   • Energy
   • Presence
   • Integrity
   • Response

   Let go of what isn't yours to carry. That's where peace begins.

7. **Shift from ownership to service:**
   When you shift from ownership to service, you become free of the conditions you put on yourself. You stop performing for approval and start moving with the alignment of value. Let your effort be an act of devotion, not desperation. Ownership comes from the place of this, which has to work very controllably and rigidly, whereas service is about it. I'm here to contribute and give the best value I can.

8. **Create Space between you and the emotion:**
    You are not your emotion—you're the observer of it. When you experience an emotion, pause, name it, and breathe. Then, choose how to respond. For example, instead of saying "I am anxious," say "I'm feeling anxious." That one word, feeling, creates distance; that space is where your power lives.

9. **Stop "shoulding" on yourself:**
    "Should" is a mental shackle that traps you in blame/shame and chains you to the past. Whereas "could" frees you to move forward. Replace your "should "with "could." For example:

    "I should be further."

    "They should've supported me."

    "It should've worked out."

    Replace "should" with "could":

    *   "I *could* be further—but I'm learning right here."
    *   "He *could* have supported me—but now I know where he stands."

10. **Anchor your purpose, not the outcome:**
    Purpose is your compass. The outcome is just the weather. When you anchor to purpose, you stay grounded. When you chase outcomes, you get tossed by the wind. You're not here to control everything but to align with what matters most.

    Ask yourself: Am I acting from purpose, or pressure?

Let your actions reflect what you believe in, not what you fear. Stay rooted in what's true, peaceful, and positive. Let the rest unfold as it will. You're not here to micromanage every moment; you're here to live by what matters most: truth, love, growth, and peace. Let your actions reflect who you are, not your fears or worries.

Thought-Provoking Question

What's one thing you need to release to make space for what truly matters?

PRINCIPLE 6

PURPOSE GIVES YOU DIRECTION

*"Hoping drains your energy.
Action creates energy."*
~ Robert Kiyosaki

Purpose doesn't just strike out of the blue, like a bolt of lightning. It's not a sudden, dramatic epiphany. It emerges in the quiet, honest moments through action, alignment, and energy.

Imagine purpose like tuning into a radio station. If you're not on the right frequency, all you get is static. But when you find the right signal, everything falls into place. It just feels right. That's what it's like when something is designed specifically for you.

Let me save you some time if you've ever wondered, "Is this person into me?" or "Does this job value me?" The answer is no if you have to ask. Energy always speaks the truth. Movement shows purpose. When it's right, it just works. You'll feel the resistance when it's not.

Don't chase after what's right for you. You don't have to beg for something that's meant for you to know your worth.

Your purpose isn't about making noise, but creating harmony with the right opportunities.

When the energy you put into something isn't coming back to you, that's a sign to change course. This isn't about proving your worth; it's about tuning in to what makes your soul light up and moving toward it.

We often get caught up in stories that keep us stuck in survival mode, thinking, "This is just how it is" or "This is all I know." But purpose breaks that cycle, giving you direction, not just movement, to encourage growth.

There's a saying I live by: Imagine holding a compass. The needle doesn't speak up or ask for anything; it points north. That's what purpose is like. It might not always tell you exactly what to do, but it'll always guide you toward the truth. Just do it. And what about when everything seems to be falling apart? That's often when everything finally comes together. It's all about your perspective.

Discovering your life's purpose doesn't have to be a struggle, and it's not about one defining moment. It's more like tuning in to it. You adjust, listen, and refine until the signal becomes clear.

Find your purpose by looking at your life, not by searching for it. What activities make you lose track of time? What topics or causes stir up strong emotions in you? What patterns keep showing up in your life, even the tough ones?

Your struggles can often make you stronger. Purpose often comes from pain. I've learned that your mess can become your message. What have you gone through, healed from, or overcome? What lessons did those challenges teach you that others still need to learn?

Discovering your purpose often comes down to what you're good at and how you can help others. The sweet spot is where your skills align with what people need. Think about what people thank you for and what comes easily to you, yet is highly valued by others.

Don't wait for permission to try something new. Purpose comes from taking action. Volunteer, create, teach, speak, travel, mentor, and reflect on each activity - did it energize you or drain you?

It's not just about what you do, but how it makes you feel while doing it. Does this path give me energy or drain me? Does it feel like I'm being pulled forward or forced to push against a resistance?

As you grow, your purpose may shift from what you wanted as a child. That's okay - just let it evolve. The person you're becoming will require a new level of purpose.

Thought-Provoking Question

Are you truly committed to this path or just going along with it?

PRINCIPLE 7

MASTER THE
FOUR PILLARS WITHIN

*"Sometimes when you get disappointment
it makes you stronger."*
~ David Rudisha

Think of your life as a four-legged chair, with your mind, body, spirit, and soul as its pillars. Many people focus on achieving results without giving these areas the attention they deserve. The world often encourages chasing outcomes without teaching us how to build a solid foundation. But just like a chair, if one of these pillars is weak or missing, you'll lose your balance and struggle to stay afloat.

When you strengthen and align each pillar, you become rooted, strong, and adaptable. You no longer fear storms; instead, you face them head-on. You don't crumble under pressure; you remain steady. The key is to start from wherever you are, and it's okay if that's not where you're meant to be. What matters is that you take the first step.

PILLAR ONE IS YOUR MIND:

Shape your ideas like a well-trained force. Direct your attention where it will do the most good. Stay alert to your thoughts, be vigilant, and develop mental resilience. Challenge your self-doubt, keep things simple, and sharpen your decision-making skills. Mental strength isn't about avoiding doubt altogether; it's about not letting it hold you back.

Train your thoughts like a disciplined unit. Mental strength isn't about never feeling uncertain—it's about not letting it take control. People with mental strength manage their emotions, thoughts, and actions with intention.

Mentally strong people:

- Take responsibility instead of wallowing in self-pity.
- Adjust to change
- Concentrate on what they can control
- Use the filter: Does this benefit me?
- Set boundaries and say no
- Learn from failure; it's just feedback.
- Celebrate others without jealousy
- Enjoy the journey, not just the reward
- Utilize solitude to understand themselves, not to isolate, but to align.

Think of your mind as the control center of your life. Sharpen it, challenge it, and protect it.

PILLAR TWO IS YOUR BODY:

Think of your body as your sanctuary and means of transport. Fuel it with whole foods, stay active, and treat it with respect. Stress and recovery can help you build resilience. By taking care of your body, you'll have the strength, health, and energy to reach your goals. Strength isn't just about size – it's about how well you bounce back. It's about recovering from stress. When you exercise, you're teaching your body to adapt. Lift, exercise, stretch, rest, and eat mindfully. Your body gets stronger when you balance effort with rest. Don't push it too far; be kind to it. This is your home for this life, so care for it properly.

PILLAR THREE IS YOUR SPIRIT:

At the heart of your being lies a calm power that brings you hope, purpose, and resilience. Though invisible, the force carries you through when your mind and body are at their weakest. Cultivating gratitude, surrender, and a connection to something greater than yourself - whether it's God, the universe, or a higher purpose - can help you develop spiritual strength. This is the inner compass that guides you when rational thinking fails and emotions cloud your judgment. If you trust that God is your source of strength, nothing that life throws your way can surpass the inner power you already possess.

PILLAR FOUR IS YOUR SOUL:

Deep down, your soul is your own divine signature, a one-of-a-kind energy that reveals who you truly are beyond the masks, distractions, and roles you play. It holds your instincts, your purpose, and the core truths about yourself. Your soul doesn't shout; it whispers in quiet moments. It speaks up when you stop pretending not to care and start tuning in. To nurture your soul, you need to think, be fully honest, accept yourself, and live the life you were meant for, not the one the world expects.

Thought-Provoking Question

Currently, which of your four pillars requires more focus—and what would shift in your life if you dedicated yourself to it?

PRINCIPLE 8

CHOOSE FAITH OVER FEAR

*"Faith is taking the first step
even when you don't see the whole staircase."*
~ Martin Luther King Jr.

Let me share a story that changed my perspective on faith: Two farmers were enduring a brutal drought. The sun scorched their fields day after day, and the sky offered nothing but silence. Their crops were dying, and their hope was dwindling. Both did what they knew to do: they prayed.

They knelt down and asked for rain. Both believed, both hoped, and repeated the same words day after day, but only one took action.

While one farmer waited for the sky to change, the other went to work. He tilled the soil, cleared the weeds, mended broken fences, and repaired his tools. He even planted new seeds during the drought.

People thought he was foolish. "Why waste your energy?" they asked. "There's no rain in sight." But he kept showing up, not because he saw the clouds, but because he believed they would come. And then one day the rain came.

Only one farmer had a field ready to receive it. So, who had more faith?

It's easy to say, "I believe." But when there's no proof yet, living your faith is a lot tougher. Faith isn't just about saying things or hoping for the best. It's about doing things that match what you believe. Faith is about getting ready. It's about putting on your boots and moving forward, even when the skies are clear.

When you live in fear, you wait. But when you live in faith, you plant. You trust that the rain will come, and when it does, you'll be ready.

Fear, doubt, and worry are like mental viruses. They drain you, make decision-making tough, and disconnect you from your true self. On the other hand, faith brings clarity. It brings you back to the present and reminds you that there's a higher power guiding the process, even when you don't have all the answers.

Kids aren't driven by fear. They have fun, play, explore, and express their happiness freely. At some point, we learned to be afraid, but that's not our natural state. Faith is. The faith that things will happen as they should.

Faith doesn't mean sitting around and doing nothing. It doesn't mean waiting for things to happen. It means doing your part and then trusting GOD, the universe, or whatever you believe in to meet you halfway. Plant your seeds, give them water, and then let go of the timeline. Everything will happen in its own time.

Here's the thing: chasing is for the dogs. You don't need to chase after people, attention, success, or love. When you know what you want and stay focused, it will come to you.

Faith is a powerful force. It's the inner flame that says, "I'll keep showing up, keep building, and keep trusting." It's about becoming the person who naturally draws in the people, opportunities, and outcomes that match your energy.

Thought-Provoking Question

What can you do today to show you're getting ready for the rain, even before the clouds roll in?

PRINCIPLE 9

LEAD WITH COMPASSION AND STRENGTH

"If fear is the great enemy of intimacy, love is its true friend."
~ Henri Nouwen

Long ago, a fierce storm tore through a valley, unleashing strong winds, heavy rain, and turmoil. Amidst the chaos, two trees stood tall: a sturdy oak and a slender bamboo.

The oak towered over the others, its branches spread out like warriors ready for battle. In contrast, the bamboo seemed fragile, bending almost to the ground with every gust of wind, yet it never broke.

The storm shattered the sturdy oak, ripping its roots and splitting its trunk. But the bamboo remained, swaying in the wind, bending without breaking. Being strong doesn't always mean being tough, and being kind doesn't always mean being weak. It's the balance of both that makes you strong and flexible, like bamboo.

Standing tall in your truth is what it means to lead with strength. Leading with kindness means being flexible with those who need it. You can't have one without the other.

People don't want a leader who's always strict and "tough." They need someone who cares and does the right thing, someone who can be calm yet firm and knows when to be strong and when to bend.

You don't have to yell to be heard.

You don't have to be in charge to earn respect.

You just need to be a leader who leads by example, with a strong sense of purpose and a big heart.

The bamboo didn't fight the storm; it went with it. It didn't break under strain; it stayed true to itself. That's the lesson.

Real Strength Isn't About Standing Rigid

It's about knowing when to stand your ground and when to let go. That's what makes a good leader. The same idea applies to intimacy, connection, and leadership: it's not about what you can get, but what you're willing to give. You can't connect if you're scared, and you can't lead if you're short on confidence. You can't love someone just because of their achievements. But you really connect with people when you lead from a place of appreciation, not expectation, and meet them where they are, not where you want them to be. That connection has power, whether it leads to something romantic or not.

Love isn't about exerting power or chasing after someone. It's about being fully present, grounded, calm, and there. Don't lead from a place of need; lead from a place of love. When you don't try to force or seize control, you make room for the right things to come your way.

Let's talk about compassion and strength now. Without one, the other isn't complete. Is it too soft? People will take advantage of you. Too hard? You'll lose your humanity. That's true power when you stand up for your values and open your heart. The mess surrounding you? You don't have to absorb it all. Take a deep breath, get your mind in the right place, and don't let the noise outside get to you.

You're the first step toward leadership, not your job title, resume, or reputation. You're a leader by who you are, even when no one's watching. Be like bamboo when you lead – planted, adaptable, and unshakeable.

Thought-Provoking Question

Where in your life can you find a balance between strength and compassion, like the bamboo, strong enough to stand on its own, but flexible enough to bend when needed?

PRINCIPLE 10

DETACH FROM THE OUTCOME

*"When you're playing your part,
you don't watch other people-
you just play your part."*
~ Ray Fearon

"Holding on doesn't make you strong. Letting go does." There's an old tale about an archer who spent years honing his stance, breathing, and form. He'd step into position every morning, focused, grounded, and calm. Every shot was clean, fluid, and on target. Then came the tournament. Now, there was status, recognition, and approval at stake. He stepped up, took aim, and missed. He tightened his grip, overthought it, and missed again. A teacher nearby said, "Your form is perfect. But your mind? It's elsewhere. You're not focused on the shot—you're fixated on the scoreboard."

That story resonated with me because that's where most of us are. We put in the work, prepare, and build consistency until the moment becomes too crucial, and then we clutch too tightly and try to control the outcome that was never in our hands. In reality, you can control your breathing and technique, but you can't control the outcome.

When you let go of the outcome, you're not giving up on effort; you're freeing yourself from emotional attachment. You're fully committed to the process, but the result doesn't define your sense of self. You show up purposefully, give it your all, and stay present not because you need a guarantee, but because it aligns with your true self. That's what true detachment means: giving everything while needing nothing in return to prove your worth. Its strength lies in surrender. It's about finding freedom in discipline. It's how you move forward without being held back by what happens.

Dr. Wayne Dyer referred to it as "letting go of the outcome to make room for the universe to work through you." Tony Robbins would say, "Live in a beautiful state no matter what's happening." Napoleon Hill taught, "Definiteness of purpose is the starting point, but faith is what keeps it going." And Buddhism says, "You only lose what you hold onto."

Before you let go, step back and ask yourself a few questions. What outcome are you holding onto? What scenario do you feel like you absolutely need to happen? Instead, write down one or two outcomes you're currently pushing for. Then, consider: If things don't go your way, can you still learn, grow, and move forward?

Focus on who you are, not what you achieve. Many people try to manifest success by chasing results, but your identity changes your life. Ask yourself: Who am I becoming through this process? Am I proud of how I'm showing up? Instead, anchor yourself in your role and the consistent, values-driven actions you take daily. Let your outcomes reflect who you are, not define you.

As Tony Robbins puts it, "Trade your expectations for appreciation and your whole life changes." And he's absolutely right. You reclaim your peace when you let go of how things should go. Expectations are future-focused attachments that tie up your energy in a specific outcome, but appreciation is about what's happening right now. It's about embracing the present and what's already working.

Detachment doesn't mean you don't care; it means you trust. You trust that your efforts matter, even if the outcome takes time. You stop needing constant validation and checking in on your progress daily. You let things unfold naturally.

Appreciation gives your efforts a solid foundation, and faith is what nourishes it.

You don't need instant results to know something powerful is happening beneath the surface. Try this: Every night, write down three things you appreciated about your efforts, not just the final result. Did you show up when you didn't feel like it? Did you move forward with integrity? Did you stay grounded when things got uncertain?

Here's the truth: Holding on tight doesn't make you strong; letting go does. Letting go doesn't mean giving up; it means stopping the struggle. It means taking a deep breath and trusting that what's meant for you won't pass you by.

Embracing a "we'll see" attitude changes your energy from control to trust. Giving up on expectations isn't about surrender but creating space. It's about living from a deeper place of surrender and strength. My dad used to say, "God willing," and he meant it with faith, not hesitation. He was releasing the need to control outcomes and trusting that life had a bigger plan. I didn't get it back then, but I do now.

I live by an old story that perfectly captures the spirit of detachment. A farmer's horse ran away, and his neighbor rushed over to say, "That's terrible!" The farmer replied, "We'll see."

A few days later, the horse returned, with three wild horses in tow. The neighbor said, "What great luck!" The farmer just nodded and said, "We'll see."

Soon after, the farmer's son broke his leg trying to tame one of the wild horses. The neighbor said, "That's awful!" The farmer replied, "We'll see."

A week later, soldiers arrived to draft young men into the war. Because of the broken leg, the farmer's son was spared. The neighbor said, "You're so lucky!" The farmer answered, "We'll see."

That's detachment, neither passivity nor indifference, but being firmly grounded and fully present. Trusting that we never truly know what something means until the story unfolds. Life is never just one moment. It's a string of unfolding events.

The very thing that feels like a setback today may turn out to be your turning point tomorrow. But if you're too fixated on labeling it as "bad," you'll miss the blessing trying to emerge. That's why the alchemist doesn't react — he observes. He watches the storm, not with fear, but with reverence. He knows that pain has purpose, delays have direction, and the bigger picture is rarely revealed in the moment.

When pressure builds, the alchemist doesn't white-knuckle his way through. He exhales. He finds his center. He stops trying to force the outcome and instead asks, *"What's the lesson here?"* Because real strength isn't about forcing your way through. It's about flowing with wisdom. It's about saying, *"If it's meant for me, it will be. And if it's not, then something better is on its way."*

You weren't placed here just to hit the target — you were put here to master the draw.

- To show up every day with intention.
- To plant the seed, water it with love, and then step back.
- To trade attachment for alignment.
- To trade expectation for appreciation.

So, the next time life throws you something unexpected, pause. Instead of labeling it, lean back and say what the farmer did — what my father always said: *"We'll see... God willing."*

That's not surrendering your power — that's stepping into it. That's how you let go... and still lead.

Thought-Provoking Question

Even if the outcome you're working towards doesn't turn out as you expected, but you become stronger, gain more clarity, and grow more aligned along the way, would it still be worthwhile?

SPEAK YOUR TRUTH, LIVE YOUR TRUTH

"There are two ways of spreading light:
to be the candle or the mirror that reflects it."
~ Edith Wharton

Picture this: you're given a compass at birth, but over time, others touch it, shaping the needle. Parents, teachers, bosses, relationships, and culture all influence you. That compass still spins when you're an adult, but it's no longer pointing north.

Here's the thing: you're on a path, but something feels off. You check the map, but the destination never feels right. Until one day, you stop, step off the trail, and hold that compass still. You wipe off the fingerprints and listen to that quiet pull inside.

That's your truth, your real direction - not the loudest voice or the most popular route.

Your truth is the only map that will truly lead you home.

Embracing Your Authentic Self: Be true to yourself, and don't change for anyone else. It's not about shouting down others; it's about being genuine. Stay true to your beliefs, even if others don't get it or walk away.

You don't owe anyone a watered-down version of yourself. You don't need to apologize for your feelings, wants, or needs. Your truth isn't for others to validate; it's for you to live.

Start here to reclaim your power:

- Be honest with yourself about your wants, needs, and desires.
- Express your feelings without shame.
- Let go of needing approval.
- Set boundaries that protect your energy.
- Stop trying to control how others see you or feel about you.
- Make your needs a priority.
- Train your mind to see clearly, not through fear or fantasy.

Here's the truth: when you live your truth, some people will leave. Let them go. Your truth doesn't need their approval; it needs your dedication.

Thought-Provoking Question

Where are you hiding your truth, and what would shift if you let it shine?

PRINCIPLE 12

CHASE GROWTH, NOT GOLD

"Not all legends are about victory.
Some are about struggle,
finding out who you are, and the reason for being."
~ Legendary (2010)

As an athlete, we train to win, to push for personal records, and to chase recognition. For a long time, I thought that was the goal. But looking back, I don't remember the medal ceremonies or the applause. What I do remember is the journey, the 5 a.m. alarms, the soreness that made it hard to walk, and the losses that broke me down. I remember the teammates who lifted me up and the days I wanted to quit but didn't. I remember the version of me who kept showing up, even when no one was watching.

That's the version I'm proud of, because the truth is, winning doesn't change you – it's the process that does. It's the daily choices, mindset, discipline, and setbacks. That's where growth happens, where purpose lives. The journey is the destination that builds character. As my coach would say, talent will get you to the top, but character is what keeps you there. We don't train to win, but to become someone we respect – someone who can handle the weight of a win or a loss with grace. We don't climb just for the summit, but because of who we become with every step.

Let me leave you with this story. There was once a young man who wanted to climb a sacred mountain. He believed that he would find wisdom, peace, purpose, and completeness at the top. So, he trained. He mapped his route. He bought the best gear. Every step was measured. Every breath was part of a plan.

Halfway up, he met an old traveler resting by a stream. "Where are you going?" the old man asked.

"To the top," the young man said with pride. "I've prepared for years. I won't stop until I get there."

The old man nodded. Then said, "I once thought the same."

"What changed?" the young man asked.

"I reached the summit," the old man said. "And all I could think was, *Why was I in such a hurry?*"

He looked around. "I missed the sound of the birds. I rushed past the wildflowers. I ignored the people I could've shared a story with. I was so focused on 'there' that I never arrived 'here.'"

He smiled. "It's not about the mountain. It's about how you walk it."

This story teaches us that we don't need to arrive to be fulfilled. Meaning is found in how we show up on our journey, not in reaching the end. Peace comes from being present, not from arriving. There's no such thing as "someday." There's only now. When we learn to appreciate each step, even the tough ones, the path becomes the purpose.

Thought-Provoking Question

What's the lesson your life is trying to teach you right now?

TRANSFORM PAIN INTO POWER

*"Do not pray for an easy life,
pray for the strength to endure a difficult one."*
~ Bruce Lee.

At one point, my body started sending me clear signals that I couldn't ignore. My nervous system was completely drained. My energy levels plummeted. Sleep became disjointed. Every decision—about food, people, and environments- helped me recover or pushed me further out of balance. This wasn't just physical pain; it was emotional, mental, and spiritual exhaustion.

I had to slow down, not because I wanted to, but because my body wouldn't let me do otherwise.

I used to try to control everything, fix it, force it, or outwork it. But this time, that didn't work. I had to pay attention, let go of control, and learn how to just be. I learned to be patient, not because I wanted to, but because I had to. And in the silence, I could finally hear myself again.

Pain became my teacher. It asked me to pay attention.

- To notice what was serving me and what wasn't.

- To observe what brought peace and what triggered stress.
- To be present, even when it was uncomfortable.

What I know today is that pain is not your enemy; it is your invitation. There is always the chance to learn something from a hurt. Inside every failure is the plan for your success.

You can turn your suffering into strength, like an alchemist turns base metals into gold. But you have to sit with it. Pay attention to it. Take lessons from it. Only then can you transform it.

Think about this: Bruce Lee stated, "Be like water." Pain teaches us to be flexible, and that's what it does. But there is another picture that helps:

Picture a sword being forged. It's placed in the fire. Then beaten. Then cooled. Over and over again. Why? Without that process, the blade would never be strong enough. That's pain. And that's power—refined, not defined by fire.

You are not free if anything in your life has control over you. You feel small, insecure, and stuck when you chase anything to feel complete. But you find your strength when you stop chasing it and face it instead of running away from it.

Thought-Provoking Question:

What's holding you back in life, and how would your future self appreciate you for facing it head-on today?

PRINCIPLE 14

FORGIVE TO BE FREE

"Man's mind and his behavior are one.
His inner thought and outer expression
cannot contradict each other."
~ Bruce Lee

Picture planting a garden in soil that's not ideal. You wouldn't expect the seeds to grow well. To help them thrive, you'd take a close look at the soil, clear out rocks and weeds, and make room for new life to take hold.

Forgiveness works in a similar way. If you're still holding onto anger, resentment, or blame, you're setting yourself up for a tough future. No matter how much attention or care you give it, anything built on anger won't flourish.

I struggled to learn this. Initially, I thought I'd done the work by letting go of the past, distancing myself from those who hurt me, and moving forward. But when my health started to decline, something deeper surfaced. I realized I wasn't just angry at them; I was also angry at myself for not being able to keep up. I needed rest, but all I knew was to push harder. And that anxiety? It was suffocating my growth.

Healing didn't begin with another treatment or supplement. It started when I forgave myself. I acknowledged that it's okay to slow down, feel my emotions, and stop trying to control everything. Forgiveness is like a detox, clearing the mental clutter so your life can grow in harmony.

The truth is, you can't cultivate what's good if you're continually feeding what's bad.

Thought-Provoking Question

Where in your life are you still planting in toxic soil—and what would change if you chose to clear it today?

PRINCIPLE 15

TAME THE VOICE WITHIN

*"It's our small voice within that is our oppressor;
it says we are not worthy and not powerful enough.
Our limited beliefs are the real foes we need to fight and conquer."*
~ Yehuda Berg

Imagine this scenario: You and a friend are sitting in a coffee shop, and someone at the next table leans over and starts yelling at them. "You're not good enough. You always mess things up. Who do you think you are to do that?" Would you sit there and let it happen? No way. You'd defend your friend, saying, "That's not true. Don't talk to them like that."

Here's the question: Why do we let that kind of self-talk run rampant inside our minds?

Why do we let our inner critic go unchecked, spreading lies and destroying our self-confidence?

The truth is, the voice in your head isn't always your own. It's a reflection of fears, failures, and hurtful comments from your past that you're still processing.

But that was then. Now, you know better, and knowing better means making a change.

You wouldn't let someone insult your closest friend.

You wouldn't let someone shame your child.

So why let that voice bully you?

Think of your mind as a garden, not a battlefield. The seeds you plant are the words you say to yourself. Weave out the negative thoughts and replace them with kindness. Overcome doubt with truth and fear with love.

Thought-Provoking Question

How would your life change if you treated yourself the way you treat the people you care about?

PRINCIPLE 16

GUARD YOUR ENERGY LIKE GOLD

"Your energy is your currency, spend it wisely."
~ Frederick A. Martinez

Be discerning with your energy. When you give your energy away, you're giving away a piece of yourself. And if you're not careful, you end up drained, resentful, and disconnected from who you really are.

Let me break it down: Ever tried to jumpstart a dead car battery? It's like a vampire – it'll drain everything from yours if you're not careful. That's why your car needs to be running while jumping it – the alternator is working to recharge what's being used.

Life works the same way. You're draining your reserves when you keep giving someone your time, energy, and validation, but they don't give you anything back. And if you're not connected to your source, rest, intention, and truth, you'll burn out.

Reflection Exercise:

Make a list. Where are you giving your energy away without return? Where are you giving compliments, attention, or validation with an attachment to being seen, liked, or responded to?

For instance, you might post a comment on social media about someone you're interested in, hoping they'll notice and respond. That's not about being generous—it's about seeking attention. It's subtle, but that seeking takes a toll, draining your energy, and if it becomes a habit, you'll find yourself running on empty.

Protecting your energy is not up for debate. You don't owe anyone unlimited access—whether to your time, peace, attention, or mind. It's essential to set boundaries, not out of anger or ego, but out of respect for yourself. Protecting your energy is about being intentional with the people, environments, habits, and thoughts you let into your life. This means saying no to things that drain you and yes to things that align with your truth. It's about taking full ownership of your energy and refusing to let it get sucked into feelings of guilt, overcommitment, or people-pleasing.

Some Boundaries to Remember:

- It's not my responsibility to fix others.
- It is perfectly acceptable to say no.
- It's not my responsibility to take care of others.
- It's not my responsibility to anticipate the needs of others.
- No one has to agree with me.
- I take responsibility for my feelings.
- I have the right to my feelings.
- I have the right to express my needs openly.

Energy Drain to Watch Out For: "Some people are writing energy checks their souls can't cash."

These habits overdraft your emotional and spiritual bank account:

- Persistent overthinking.
- Holding onto the past.
- Being around negative people.

- Consuming a large amount of processed foods.
- Inconsistent sleep patterns.
- Taking things personally.
- Living in the future.
- People-pleasing
- Gossiping
- Complaining
- Experiencing excessive stress
- Fueling the drama
- Comparing yourself with others
- Constantly scrolling through social media.
- Negative self-talk.
- Avoiding the present moment.
- Seeking for validation.
- Jealousy and envy.

Remember, you always have a say in who you give your energy to, what you put up with, and how you react when people show you their true colors. Think of your energy like a water tank in your home. It's limited, needs pressure, and requires direction. But if you've got faucets dripping all day—people who drain your attention, peace, and time—you'll eventually wake up completely drained. That's what happens when you give energy to people or situations that aren't flowing freely in return. You don't feel inspired; you feel exhausted, and that's the sign.

There are three things you should never have to plead for:

- Someone to be a part of your life.
- Someone to open up to.
- Someone's time and attention.

If it's not offered freely, stop chasing. You're not a beggar for connection; you're the gatekeeper of your energy.

True power in action is about taking charge of your choices. It's not about controlling others, but about setting clear boundaries and protecting your emotional well-being.

By redirecting your energy from draining situations, you can focus on what truly matters. This isn't about being selfish—it's about gaining clarity. When you prioritize yourself, you become more captivating. You stop settling for less because you realize you've been the main attraction all along.

Thought-Provoking Question

Where are you giving your power away, and what would it look like to put yourself first instead?

PRINCIPLE 17

PRACTICE RADICAL
SELF-ACCEPTANCE

*"If you don't stand your ground,
then all that happens is people push you backwards."*
~ Jordan Peterson.

Imagine standing in front of a mirror that reflects your face and your entire story, including every scar, every mistake, and every time you felt like you weren't good enough, weren't seen, or weren't enough. But also, every win, every time you stood back up, and every time you persevered even when no one was watching. Most people tend to show only the best parts, hiding the flaws, blurring the pain, and downplaying the noise.

Radical self-acceptance is about facing yourself in the mirror and saying, "This is me, with all my flaws." You're not seeking approval from others. It's like nurturing a bonsai tree - you don't criticize it for growing slowly or judge its curves. You appreciate every twist and turn because it has a story to tell. A tree that's been shaped by storms, seasons, and time still stands tall. You're no different - you weren't meant to be perfect but whole and complete.

Radical self-acceptance isn't about stopping growth; it's the foundation that allows growth to thrive. You can't grow from shame, only from love. This isn't about settling for less but embracing your whole self. It's about understanding who you are, what you value, and what you won't compromise on. You don't need to earn your worth; you're worthy right now, not when you've achieved more, lost weight, or fixed every flaw.

Self-acceptance is a quiet movement that says, "I'm already enough, and I'm still growing." Like a tree, the stronger your roots, the higher you'll rise.

Thought-Provoking Question

How would your life be different if you stopped trying to change yourself and started embracing the person you are right now?

PRINCIPLE 18

MEET YOURSELF
IN THE MIRROR

"Stand up and face your fears, or they will defeat you."
~ LL Cool J.

Standing in front of the mirror is like stepping into the ring—except you're not fighting someone else, but the version of yourself you've been dodging. It's facing your reflection head-on, no hiding. Not the version you present to the world, but the real one. The one that remembers every doubt, every scar, every time you said you'd try tomorrow.

It's tempting to look away, to flinch. But when the lights are on and there's no crowd, just you and the truth, you either face it or fake it.

Here's the thing: you can't heal what you won't see. You can't lead others if you don't look at your reflection. The mirror doesn't lie, but it doesn't shame either. It just reveals. And when you face it with courage—not ego, not fear—you stop fighting yourself, running, and start rebuilding. Stronger, cleaner, real.

The mirror becomes your guide, not to judge, but to awaken.

Facing the mirror means being brutally honest with yourself. No filters, no blaming, no hiding behind your story. You can't change what you won't confront. If you want to grow, heal, and rise, you've got to look yourself in the eye and call it what it is.

Your habits, fears, excuses, self-talk—all of it. The mirror doesn't lie, but it doesn't judge either. It just reflects what's there. Your job is to have the courage to see it and then take action to shift it.

Fear is rooted in your mind, not always real, but it always feels real. Some say FEAR means Forget Everything and Run, others say Face Everything and Rise. I've got another version: Fun Every Day And Rejoice. It sounds bold, but that's what it takes. Live your life fully, show up, take risks, and reclaim the joy.

When you avoid fear, it owns you; you take your power back when you face it.

With everything happening right now, this is the perfect time to get straight with yourself. Let go of self-blame, the "I should've done more," "I could've been farther along," "Why didn't it work out?" stories.

That kind of thinking keeps you stuck in the past. You can't rewrite history, but you can choose what you do now.

Ask yourself: What can I learn from this moment? What is this season trying to teach me?

Take a moment to reflect on your feelings right now, without holding back. What's on your mind? What's in your heart? You're here for a reason. Something valuable is waiting to be learned, and it's meant just for you.

Looking at yourself in the mirror can be easy, but seeing yourself clearly is a challenge. The alchemist is brave enough to look within and face the patterns, pain, and truths that are hiding in plain sight.

There's power in taking full responsibility—not to blame, but to drive change. What you don't own will control you. The mirror shows you where you are and where you're avoiding. Face it with courage, not judgment.

Thought-Provoking Question:

What risk are you glad you took, and what fear did you have to face to get there?

PRINCIPLE 19

SLOW DOWN
TO SPEED UP

"Do not speak bad of yourself.
For the warrior within hears your words
and is lessened by them"
~ Old Japanese Samurai Proverb

When life gets chaotic, our natural response is to push harder, work more, and look for answers outside ourselves. But genuine clarity doesn't come from doing more—it comes from quieting down. Inner alchemy isn't about achieving more; it's about finding balance. It begins by slowing down just enough to tune in to what's off inside you—your thoughts, your breath, your energy—and bringing them back into harmony. That's when real transformation starts. When you take a moment to pause, everything begins to change. You step out of fight-or-flight mode and back into presence:

- Your breath realigns with your intention
- Your thoughts begin to reflect your purpose
- Your actions reconnect with your truth

That's how you recalibrate. That's how you regain your power.

Imagine your body and mind like a high-performance sports car. When everything is in sync, the ride is smooth, efficient, and powerful. But if the wheels are even slightly off, the ride gets rough, no matter how much you accelerate. The car starts to drift, wears out faster, and you start blaming the road. Most people keep pushing, thinking motion will fix the discomfort. But the car doesn't need more speed—it needs a break in the garage, a moment to recalibrate.

You're that mechanic. Your breath, stillness, and reset are your garage. Slowing down is how you stop grinding and start gliding.

This is the art of inner alchemy—refining your life's raw energy through presence and intention until everything hums again.

We live in a world full of distractions, excess, and noise. Yet, clarity doesn't come from more—it comes from less. Want to recalibrate your life? Simplify it.

Here's what Buddhist monks have taught for generations—and what still applies today:

- Do everything with purpose
- Train your mind to see things as they are—not through ego or illusion
- Eat to nourish your body—not to numb emotions
- Wear clothing to protect you—not to impress others
- Use each space for what it's designed for—a bedroom is for sleep and intimacy, not scrolling or stress
- Use technology to share ideas—not for validation, vanity, or status

Alignment isn't about perfection. It's about **intentionality**.

The world moves quickly, but your soul moves slowly. You're not a machine; you're a rhythm, a breath, a pulse. When you slow down, you return to your natural state. You notice more, feel deeper, and align. Rushing through life may seem productive, but it robs you of presence. The alchemist doesn't confuse speed with effectiveness; he understands that alignment, not urgency, creates true impact.

Thought-Provoking Question:

What areas of your life need to slow down so you can reconnect with your true self?

Principle 20

Raise Your Vibration

"Everything in life is vibration."
~ Albert Einstein

Think of your energy like a hot air balloon. It doesn't just take off on a whim; it rises when the fire within you is clear, aligned, and has purpose. But many of us are weighed down by sandbags: past pain, negative thoughts, draining relationships, and habits that hold us back. Then we wonder why we feel stuck and heavy.

To lift your vibration, you need to be honest about what's holding you back and be willing to let go. You don't rise by force; you rise by releasing what's holding you down. Let your purpose be your driving force, and your ideas fuel your journey. Let go of the baggage that's been keeping you from being your true self. You don't need anything else; you just need to shed what's not you.

As you live at a higher frequency, everything starts to change. You attract what aligns with your true self. Opportunities come your way, and you feel better physically, mentally, and emotionally. But what does it mean to "raise your vibration"?

It means becoming the person you're meant to be, shedding the weight of your past, and embracing your purpose. It's about living in harmony with yourself, surrounded by people and experiences that resonate with your true self. It's about finding your inner fire and letting it guide you towards a life of growth and fulfillment. Let's break it down.

Low Vibration Feels Like:

- Living in despair, desperation, or constant stress
- Taking things personally
- People-pleasing
- Complaining about everything
- Holding onto the past
- Overthinking and overstressing
- Gossiping
- Creating unnecessary drama
- Poor diet, poor sleep
- Not living in the present moment

These habits drain your energy and reduce your frequency. As a result, you may feel heavy, reactive, disconnected, and stuck.

High Vibration Feels Like:

- Personal power
- Clarity
- Peace
- Love
- Joy
- A deep sense of gratitude
- A connection to something bigger than yourself

You feel light, centered, creative, present, and energized.

12 Habits to Raise Your Vibration

1. **Gratitude**
   Gratitude instantly lifts your energy. Take a moment to pause and find one thing around you to be thankful for. It transforms everything.

2. **Love**
   Love is one of the highest vibrational states. Picture someone you truly care about and feel your chest warm up.

3. **Generosity**
   One of the fastest ways to feel abundant is by giving your time, love, kindness, and service to others. The more you give, the more you'll have.

4. **Meditation & Breathwork**
   These practices help you stay present. They calm your nervous system and raise your energy level fast.

5. **Forgiveness**
   Refusing to let go of blame keeps your energy low. Forgiveness isn't about excusing the behavior; it's about freeing yourself from it.

6. **Eat High-Vibe Food**
   Whole, nutrient-dense foods boost your life force energy. You are what you consume—so eat with awareness.

7. **Eliminate Toxins**
   Alcohol, junk food, and too much stimulation cloud your clarity. Cut out what dulls your shine.

8. **Positive Thoughts**
What you focus on grows. Choose thoughts that empower you, fill you with gratitude, or spark curiosity, rather than ones that drag you down.

9. **High-Vibe Media**
Keep an eye on what you consume, whether it's music, movies, or social media. All of these can impact your mood.

10. **Surround Yourself with Beauty**
Clear out clutter and create a calm atmosphere. Light a candle, add some color, or bring in a touch of nature to make your space feel special. Surrounding yourself with beauty can really uplift your mood.

11. **Spend Time Outside**
Being outside in the fresh air, basking in sunlight, and getting some movement—this is what really heals. Spending just 10 minutes outdoors can lift your mood and recharge your energy.

12. **Choose Uplifting Relationships**
Surround yourself with people who uplift you, not drain you. Positive energy is infectious. Vibration is more than just a concept – it's your inner state. You can sense it in a room, in a conversation, and within yourself. Elevating your vibration isn't about being perfect; it's about being mindful and choosing what energizes you.

Elevating your vibration means living with gratitude, moving your body, speaking your truth, and breathing with intention. It's not just a spiritual practice; it's a strategic one. The higher your vibration, the clearer your intuition becomes, and the stronger your signal to what's truly beneficial for you.

Thought-Provoking Question:

What habits bring down your energy, and what would shift if you started elevating your frequency every day?

Principle 21

We Rise Together

"When you stop comparing what is right here and now with what you wish were, you can begin to enjoy what is."
~ Cheri Huber

Once, I thought competition meant beating the person next to you at all costs to win the gold. But during the Master's World Cup, where I represented Team USA in Olympic weightlifting, I had an epiphany. We all wore the same flag, yet part of me still saw my teammates as the enemy—until I caught myself.

My perspective shifted. I used to think success was about being on top, beating everyone else to the finish line. But I've realized that life isn't a competition, it's a path we walk together. Sure, we're all on our own paths, but we're not here to compete against each other. We're here to grow together. Now, I gauge my success by how well I work with others, not just by my achievements.

So I cheered for my teammates instead of playing mind games. I encouraged them to give their all. Because when they showed up at their best, it brought out the best in me. That's the power of collaboration over competition. It's not about dimming your light; it's about creating so much light that everyone in the room rises to the occasion.

When you stop seeing life as a scoreboard, you free yourself. You surround yourself with people who don't want to beat you; they want to work with you. And that's the winning that lasts.

Collaboration isn't about compromising or giving up your unique strengths. It's about sharpening each other, like iron sharpens iron. When you surround yourself with people who share your pursuit of excellence, you don't have to compete with them to succeed; you rise together. You motivate one another, help each other spot blind spots, and celebrate each other's successes. And when you stumble, they don't laugh; they reach down and help you back up. Real collaboration multiplies your potential. You become more than you could've been on your own, because you tapped into the power of "we" instead of "me."

Thought-Provoking Question:

Who in your life encourages you to grow, and how can you collaborate with them rather than competing against them?

PRINCIPLE 22

ASK BETTER QUESTIONS, LIVE A BETTER LIFE

*"The quality of your life is determined
by the quality of the questions you ask."*
~ Tony Robbins

Most people walk through life asking the wrong questions.

They say:

- "Why does this always happen to me?"
- "What's wrong with me?"
- "Why can't I catch a break?"

Those questions don't foster growth—they lead to a dead end. It's like driving with your GPS set to keep you stuck in a rut. You'll keep circling the same emotional block, the same limiting beliefs, the same identity. But when you start asking empowering questions, your entire direction shifts. You stop reacting and start evolving. Try asking:

- "What is life trying to teach me here?"
- "How can I grow through this experience?"
- "Who do I need to become to handle this situation easily?"

Picture your mind as a cave. Inside, you'll find your thoughts, memories, fears, and dreams—everything. The questions you ask are like a flashlight. If you ask, "Why is it always dark in here?" you'll stay stuck. But if you ask, "What's the path forward?" or "What's the next step I can take?" you'll start to notice a trail, a glimpse of light in the distance, and maybe even an exit. Your question doesn't change the cave itself; it changes what you focus on, and that changes everything.

Your questions shape your mindset, and your mindset shapes your life. If you want better results, don't ask for better answers; start asking better questions. You won't find empowerment through blame. You'll find it through taking responsibility, being curious, and having courage. That's where transformation starts—not when you have everything figured out, but when you're brave enough to ask for something better.

Thought-Provoking Question:

What's one question you've been asking yourself that's holding you back, and what's a more empowering question you could ask instead?

PRINCIPLE 23

STILLNESS IS YOUR SUPERPOWER

"You don't have to control your thoughts.
You just have to stop letting them control you."
~ Dan Millman

Ever scooped up water from a lake or river? At first, it's murky and you can't see through it. But if you just let it sit, the mud settles and what's left is clear. That's what happens with your mind too.

When you're worried, anxious, or overthinking, you might feel like you need to fix it. But the more you try to control it, the cloudier it gets. Sometimes, all your mind needs is stillness. Don't force it or judge it – just let it settle. Give it time, space, and silence. That's where wisdom emerges and answers live, beneath the noise.

Life will throw curveballs, people will test you, and situations will spiral out of control. But how you respond is your power. Stillness doesn't mean doing nothing; it means not reacting from fear, ego, or emotional chaos. It means staying centered, not scattered, and clear, not frantic. It means learning to respond, not just react. Peace is something you build, not just hope for. The more you train yourself to live from that space, the less power outside noise has over you.

To live a peaceful life, remind yourself of these truths:

- Let go of your past so it doesn't hold you back in the present.
- It's none of your business what others think of you.
- Give yourself space to heal—it's okay to take your time.
- Don't compare or judge—they've had a different journey.
- It's okay to not have all the answers.
- Only you have the power to unlock your happiness.
- Smiling can make your day (and someone else's) a whole lot brighter.

Thought-Provoking Question

What if you stopped trying to clear your mind and just let it settle?

BE FULLY PRESENT

"Gratitude unlocks the fullness of life.
It turns what we have into enough, and more.
It turns denial into acceptance, chaos to order, confusion to clarity.
It can turn a meal into a feast, a house into a home,
a stranger into a friend."
~ Melody Beattie

Being fully present is like having all your feet on the ground. You don't need to be barefoot to feel it; you just need to pay attention. Your shoes don't determine your presence; your awareness does. When you're truly grounded, you feel every subtle movement: the shift in pressure from heel to toe, how your toes adjust and respond, and the energy transfer through every small muscle in your feet.

That's your body talking—and most people miss it because they're in their heads, thinking about the past or the future, rushing or distracted. But when you slow down and focus on the present, you regain your power. Your steps become intentional, energized, and grounded. You stop coasting through life and start moving with purpose. Being fully present isn't just a mindset; it's a total body experience. It's allowing your nervous system to breathe, giving your thoughts a break, and being right here, with everything you've got.

Presence isn't just about slowing down; it's about being in tune with your surroundings. It's about genuinely occupying the space you're in, rather than being caught up in the past or rushing into the future. It's about being here and now. The quickest way to achieve presence is through gratitude, which redirects your focus to what's real, working well, and already available. This practice calms your mental chatter and opens your heart. You don't need a fancy routine; just be mindful.

Gratitude changes your energy, bringing clarity and helping you find your footing. Use this gratitude list whenever you need to get centered:

There's no rule—use it daily, weekly, or just when life feels off. Just pick one and go.

- Three qualities that make you unique.
- Three people for whom you're grateful and why.
- Three things for which you're thankful.
- A challenging experience that strengthened you.
- Three ways to incorporate gratitude into a current situation.
- When was the last time you did something kind?
- A fear you have conquered.
- Three activities you enjoy and why.
- What made you smile today?
- Three things you appreciate about your family.
- Your favorite place and the reasons for it.
- Three things you appreciate about yourself and why.
- The last time you felt overwhelming joy.
- A risk you took that you are thankful for.
- Three everyday items you value.
- Three songs that bring you happiness.
- A skill for which you are grateful.
- A luxury you appreciate.
- A rejection for which you're thankful.

- Three things about your body that you're grateful for.
- What are you most grateful for in your daily life?
- Three things you're thankful for about your home.
- Three items in your home that you're thankful for.
- Thank someone right now.
- Something in nature that gives you peace.
- A person from your past who assisted you.
- Something about work that you're grateful for.
- When was the last time you really laughed?
- Your greatest achievement.
- Three things you wish to manifest.

Appreciate the small things: Life is just a bunch of atoms bouncing around right here, right now. The fact that you're alive, reading this, and breathing isn't a coincidence. It's a statistical miracle that you were even conceived. So, don't take it for granted - every moment counts. Don't rush through life so fast that you miss what you're meant to experience in this moment.

Thought-Provoking Question:

What would shift in your life if you brought that level of attention and presence to every step, every move you make?

DON'T PLAY BY THE RULES – MAKE THEM

"Learn the rules like a pro,
so you can break them like an artist."
~ Pablo Picasso

Unless you create your own rules, someone else will decide them for you. There's a script that most people follow without even realizing it. It's been handed to you since childhood through school, culture, religion, media, and family. This script tells you what's "right," what's "realistic," and what's "safe." So you keep your head down, do what's expected, follow the path laid out for you, and maybe, just maybe, you'll be rewarded down the line.

But the truth is, nobody wants to admit it: that path was never meant to set you free—it was meant to keep you in check. As in Outwitting the Devil, the enemy isn't some grand, dramatic villain. It's distraction, drift, and losing sight of your own rules to the point where you forget you ever had them.

Most people aren't truly stuck—they're just stuck in systems they never questioned.

Don't just watch from the sidelines. You're meant to be the author of your own story. So pick up the pen and write it your way. Stop waiting for permission or approval. Don't let outdated rules, self-doubt, or other people's expectations hold you back from achieving your full potential.

Think of The Matrix. Neo is given a choice: take the blue pill and stay in the comfort of illusion, or take the red pill and wake up to the harsh reality. You face the same choice every day. The blue pill means staying small, being liked, and following the rules. The red pill means questioning everything, speaking your mind, and making your own rules.

Here's the thing: most people prefer familiarity over freedom. They'd rather have comfort than clarity. That's why they get stuck.

Understandable. As an athlete, I was conditioned to play by the rules. As an engineer, I was taught to break down the system. But at some point, I realized: if I wanted to live life to the fullest, not just exist, I had to redefine the game.

Some of the biggest legends didn't just win—they rewrote the rules. Michael Jordan didn't just play basketball—he transformed the game. Serena Williams didn't just dominate, she redefined strength and elegance. Tom Brady didn't just play longer; he broke every age barrier we thought was possible. They didn't wait to be chosen. They chose themselves. And they forced the world to adapt.

At one point in my life, I was just going through the motions, checking boxes to get by. Promotions were few and far between, and my creativity was stifled. Deep down, I felt like I was living someone else's life.

That's when I asked myself a question that shattered the illusion:

- Who wrote these rules I keep following?
- And why the hell am I letting them define me?

I stopped asking for permission. I started carving my own path. I changed how I approached engineering. I brought coaching and leadership into the room. I used mindset tools where others only saw technical tasks. I realized: the most fulfilled, impactful people in the world aren't reckless — they're *rule makers*. They study the system, then rewire it.

And here's what I've learned: The people who shape the world don't follow blindly. They analyze the system, then they bend it, break it, and rebuild it. They don't need recognition to take action. They don't need a guaranteed outcome to believe. They act because they must—because they know their identity.

Here's what you can do instead:

1. Examine the rules you're following. Ask yourself: Who set these rules? Are they helping me grow or holding me back? Write them down, then decide which ones to let go.

2. Develop your own code of conduct. Choose 3–5 principles that guide your life, based on your values, not others' expectations. Display them where you'll see them every day.

3. Practice taking bold action without asking permission. Start with one area of your life, such as career, health, or relationships. Where are you waiting for approval? Stop waiting, decide, and move forward. Let courage, not consensus, lead the way.

You weren't born to follow the rules but to create them. Nobody's going to hand you freedom; you have to take it. The world isn't waiting for permission—why are you?

Thought-Provoking Question:

What unspoken rules currently run your life, and who benefits if you keep following them?

LET PRESSURE SHAPE, NOT BREAK YOU

"Fire is the test of gold; adversity, of strong men."
~ Seneca

Pressure is a natural part of life, but how you react to it defines who you are. A lot of people try to run from pressure, viewing it as a threat to be beaten or avoided at all costs. But pressure itself isn't the real problem. The issue lies in our perception of it. Here's the thing: pressure doesn't break you; it reveals what's inside you. And if you let it, it can build you into someone stronger, sharper, and more resilient than you ever thought possible.

Think about boiling water. It's just water until you apply heat. Then everything changes. Under pressure, the water transforms. It cooks the food, softens what's hard, sterilizes what's impure, and brings hidden flavor to the surface. That same water can either harden an egg or soften a potato, depending on what's inside.

Same goes for you. Pressure doesn't decide your outcome; your inner self does. When life gets tough with deadlines, expectations, heartbreak, health scares, and financial stress, you can choose: Will this moment make you stronger or crumble you? Or will it reveal your true self, strength, and character?

I've learned to stop asking, "Why is this happening to me?" Instead, I ask, "What is this developing in me?"

What can you learn from pressure?

- Pressure is a form of feedback. It reveals your strengths and weaknesses, showing where you need to improve.
- Pressure is a form of preparation. It prepares you for what you've been striving for.
- Pressure is a privilege. It means you're in motion, pushing yourself to become something greater.

Nothing grows in comfort. Comfort doesn't mold leaders. Pressure does. So the next time you feel overwhelmed, remember this: You prayed for growth. You asked for greatness. This is where you're being shaped.

Thought-Provoking Question:

How have past pressures influenced you, and how might today's challenges be preparing you for the future you envision?

PRINCIPLE 27

REWRITE THE SCRIPT, RECLAIM YOUR POWER

"Resilience is, of course, necessary for a warrior.
But a lack of empathy isn't."
~ Phil Klay

Let me share a real-life story that most of us can relate to. Imagine your life as a movie. Now picture yourself sitting in the front row, watching your story unfold on the screen. The early scenes? They're tough to watch. Maybe you were misunderstood, got knocked down, or made a mistake. Whatever it is, that scene keeps playing repeatedly: same choices, same regrets, same ending.

You know it by heart, but you keep watching it. Here's the twist: You're not just the audience. You're the writer, director, and lead actor. And every time you replay those old scenes without changing anything, you're not just remembering the pain—you're reliving it. At some point, you've got to get out of that front-row seat, move behind the camera, and start editing the script. You don't erase what happened, but you choose what the next chapter looks like. You decide who you become because of it.

Your past isn't your punishment. It's your raw material. But if you keep letting old scenes define you, you'll never write the ending

91

you deserve. You get one shot at this life, so don't waste it by allowing old footage to play on repeat. Take the pen. Call "cut." Start the rewrite.

Thought-Provoking Question

Imagine your life as a movie—what scene are you ready to rewrite, starting now?

PRINCIPLE 28

FREE THINKERS
BREAK THE SYSTEM

"As long as you're alive, you're free. Don't let anyone box you in and tell you how to be. You can be anything you want. Free thinkers challenge the systems and institutions. They're afraid of what they can't control, and you were never meant to be held back."
~ Frederick A. Martinez

You were conditioned to fit into a box as soon as you were born. You're born, placed in a crib, and from there, it's a life spent in confinement. You go to school in a box, stare at screens in a box, drive to work in a box, and sit in a cubicle box. You even eat lunch from a box. When you get home, you scroll through ideas in a digital box, watch programs in a box, and when it's all over, you're buried in a box. Throughout your life, you're surrounded by systems designed to keep you contained – mentally, emotionally, and spiritually. These institutions, governments, religions, corporations, and algorithms want more than just your attention; they want your obedience.

As Napoleon Hill said in "Outwitting the Devil," the opposition wins by making you drift off course, not through force, but by instilling fear, creating routines, and discreetly influencing your behavior. You're led to follow the "right path," which ironically looks just like everyone else's. Think, obey, consume, sleep, and repeat.

But here's the thing: the system is strongest when you think your life has only one path, and they control the keys. The truth is, as long as you're alive, you're free. You don't have to fit into the box they've set up for you. You don't have to become what they want you to be. You can shatter every mold they try to impose on you into.

When you start thinking for yourself, really thinking, you become a threat. You start asking questions, noticing flaws in the system, and realizing that much of what you were taught was brainwashing. And that scares them. Because people who think for themselves can't be controlled. You can't be led, manipulated, or swayed by noise when grounded in your own truth.

They try to label you to keep you in line, saying you're too much, too intense, too quiet, too loud, too ambitious, too weird. But that's not who you are. You're awake. And the world doesn't know how to handle someone who can't be confined.

Your power comes from being free to question, choose, break cycles, and become whoever you want to be, not what others expect. You don't owe anyone a label, your silence, or a version of yourself that makes them comfortable.

Thought-Provoking Question

Where in your life have you let the system dictate who you are — and what would change if you finally broke free and took back control?

PRINCIPLE 29

BE THE ARCHITECT OF YOUR LIFE

"Someone once told the definition of Hell:
The last day you have on earth,
the person you became
will meet the person
you could have become"
~ Anonymous

Imagine this: you're in a dark theater, and the screen comes alive with the life you could've had - the love, the peace, the purpose, the power. You can sense it, but can't reach out and touch it. You're just a bystander, watching the best version of yourself live the life you were meant for. That's what purgatory feels like - being stuck, forced to watch it replay over and over. You don't end up there by chance - you end up there by waiting, holding back, blaming the world instead of taking control and writing your own story.

Let's be honest: victims wait for change, but creators make it happen. You're not stuck, you're not too late, and you're not broken. You have one shot, one life. So, stop watching and start creating.

Creating the life you want isn't about having it all figured out. It's about being intentional with the life you're building and the person you're becoming. Start by building a solid foundation and discovering your values. Ask yourself: What truly matters to me? Your values serve as your guiding light. If you're unsure about them, you'll lose your way.

Now, map out your vision and create a clear blueprint for your life. What do you want it to look and feel like? Be as detailed as possible. Write it down, speak it out loud, and make it a reality. Vague goals lead to vague results.

Choose the right tools to form better habits. Your habits shape your path. Small daily actions add up to big dreams with real results. Let go of what no longer serves you. If it drains, dulls, or takes you off track, it's time to move on. Growth demands space to breathe. Know your why - your purpose and what drives you. It's not something you're given, but something you discover by asking: Who benefits when I bring my full self to the table?

Imagine your life as a custom-built home. You can either design it with intention, choosing the layout, foundation, and natural light, or live in someone else's creation and wonder why it never feels right.

One path leads to peace, while the other brings frustration. You don't need permission; you need a plan and the courage to see it through. You weren't born to fit into someone else's mold but to create something unique. You don't need to chase perfection; you need to build a life that matters - one that reflects your values, your spirit, and your natural pace.

Thought-Provoking Question

What areas of your life still feel like they were designed by someone else, and what would they look like if you were to design them for yourself?

PROTECT
YOUR SACRED CIRCLE

*"Relationships are like music: never make music with anybody
who doesn't understand, appreciate and value your lyrics."*
~ Dr. Billy Alsbrooks

Think of your inner circle like your home. You wouldn't leave your front door wide open for just anyone to walk in. You wouldn't let people track dirt through your space, touch your valuables, or mess with your furniture. You'd invite those who bring peace, not chaos - the kind of people who respect your space and take off their shoes.

Your energy works the same way. The people closest to you should lift your spirits, not bring you down. They should push you to grow, not try to compete with you. They shouldn't hold you back, but hold you accountable. You don't have to shut others out to keep your circle sacred; it's about being intentional. You're not better than anyone else but should protect your peace, purpose, and growth. Let people earn their way in. Let their energy speak louder than their appearance. Remember, your circle is like soil - what grows in you depends on your surroundings.

Key Principles for Healthy Relationships:

- Don't hand out your trust—make people earn it.
- Listen more than you speak—keep two ears open and one mouth shut.
- Focus on what matters most—beyond status and looks, it's integrity, kindness, and humility that truly endure.
- Respect and love should be a two-way street.
- Genuine relationships are built over time—they're slow to develop, not rushed.
- Don't waste your energy on the wrong people—you only have so much to give.
- Some people come into your life for a reason, others for a season, and a select few for a lifetime—know the difference.
- Girls—know what your cookies are worth. If the Girl Scouts do, you should too.

Guard your inner circle. This means safeguarding your energy, peace, and purpose. Don't chase after people who can't see your value. And don't diminish yourself to fit into spaces you've outgrown. The sun doesn't dim its light for anyone, nor should you.

For many people, it's not until they're part of something bigger than themselves that they truly understand what a real connection is. In the military, your unit is like family - your teammates are like brothers and sisters. When life gets tough, your church community is there to support you. It's not about blood ties; it's about sharing the same values, respecting each other, and being there for one another. A real family doesn't just happen by accident - it takes time to build trust, consistency, and a shared goal.

When people work together, they make progress. But when they act in their own self-interest, things fall apart. The people you surround yourself with shape who you become. You become like the people you spend time with. Choose friends who know where they're headed. Look for people who are honest, keep their promises, and don't cross your boundaries. Find people who cheer you on when you succeed and hold you to your highest standard. It's better to walk alone than be lost among people who are going nowhere.

When you hang out with the wrong crowd, people will judge you, and soon, you'll start to act like them. Don't trade your peace or purpose for a false sense of belonging. Keep your circle tight and safe - it matters for your future.

Thought-Provoking Question

Who in your life brings value, and who's taking up more of your time and resources than they're worth?

PRINCIPLE 31

FUEL OTHERS TO FUEL YOURSELF

*"Thousands of candles can be lit from a single candle,
and the life of the candle will not be shortened."*
~ Buddha

We've been told to hustle, grind, and guard our energy as it's scarce. However, here's the truth that most people don't realize until they've been burned out and broken: You don't lose energy by giving it. You create energy by giving it intentionally.

Imagine yourself as a campfire. You're lit, radiating warmth, glow, and heat. Now, envision others around you—cold, struggling to find their spark. You can use your flame to ignite their fire. And guess what? Your flame doesn't diminish; in fact, it grows. When you help ignite someone else with encouragement, truth, support, or inspiration, you add wood to your own fire. Their fire nourishes yours, but here's the key: not all giving nourishes you. Fueling others isn't about draining yourself trying to save people who aren't even holding a match. It's about pouring into those ready to rise with your words, energy, and example.

How to Fuel Others to Fuel Yourself

- Share your experiences, not just your accomplishments. Others won't relate to your perfection—they'll connect with how you got there.
- Be a mirror, not a rescuer. Reflect someone's greatness back to them without trying to change them.
- Be there for them, not just offer advice. Sometimes people don't need answers—they need to feel seen and supported.
- Embracing others doesn't mean downplaying yourself. When someone else shines, it doesn't detract from your light. You're all on the same team, not competing against each other.
- Be a mentor when you're just one step ahead. You don't need to have it all figured out. If you're a chapter ahead, share the key points.

Thought-Provoking Question

Who could be inspired just by hearing your story—and what might happen to you if you were to share it?

PRINCIPLE 32

TRUST DIVINE TIMING

"Your journey has molded you for your greater good,
and it was exactly what it needed to be.
Don't think you've lost time.
It took each and every situation
you have encountered
to bring you to the present.
And now is right on time."
~ Asha Tyson

Divine timing isn't about waiting around; it's about doing the work in the meantime. Your job is to stay prepared mentally, emotionally, physically, spiritually, and financially so you can trust that everything is unfolding exactly as it should.

When you're impatient, it means you're not trusting the process. Everything has time, including love, healing, growth, and breakthroughs. To trust divine timing, you have to surrender. This means doing what you can, releasing control, and having faith in the process. It means understanding that your planted seeds are still growing, even if they're not visible yet.

Trusting divine timing is like showing up early at the airport. You've packed your bags, booked your ticket, and made it through security. Now you're at the gate, but the plane isn't ready yet. You don't rush the jet bridge or scream at the pilot

103

to take off. You wait, prepared. You trust that the call to board will come when it's time. Why? Because you've done your part: packed your bags and brought your ID. Now it's the airline's turn to do their job.

This is divine timing. You don't just sit around at the gate; you stay prepared. You drink water, stretch, and review your itinerary. You're ready to go when the call comes, and you don't have to worry about being on the wrong plane.

Here's the message: get ready as if it's already happening. Assume the plane is full and be patient, knowing your seat has already been taken care of. Divine timing isn't just about waiting around—it's about staying productive while you wait. When you trust that everything is unfolding as it should, your task is to stay prepared mentally, emotionally, physically, spiritually, and financially.

Ways to Invest in Yourself:

- Engage in daily exercise.
- Eat clean by avoiding processed sugars and fried foods.
- Learn how to cook.
- Forgive others—and yourself.
- Stop looking for approval.
- Participate in self-improvement seminars
- Watch educational videos, listen to podcasts, and listen to audiobooks.
- Read books, acquire new skills, and enroll in online courses.
- Develop an investment plan
- Develop a savings and spending plan (emergency fund, vacation fund, bills)
- Choose your friends wisely
- Let go of toxic people.
- Begin a business

- Seek a mentor
- Learn a language.
- Set goals and plan your days.
- Engage in meditation and cultivate gratitude
- Create a life plan
- Begin a hobby
- Get enough sleep—6 to 8 hours.
- Maintain a routine
- Travel more, and experience more.
- Challenge yourself every day
- Invest in experiences rather than material possessions.
- Envision your definition of success.
- Don't be concerned about what others think.
- Stop putting things off.
- Manage your time as if it matters—because it does.

Thought-Provoking Question

What's one area of your life where you need to let go of control and have more faith?

PRINCIPLE 33

BECOME WHO
YOU WERE BORN TO BE

*"Everybody has their story – at some point you have to say,
'This is who I am: now it's up to me to become what I want to be."*
~ Monica Seles.

For much of our lives, we try to fit the mold others have set for us. We aim to make our parents proud, meet society's expectations, and be who we think we should be. But the reality is, you weren't meant to blend in—you were meant to stand out. You're one-of-a-kind, just like a fingerprint. Nobody else was made like you. And only God knows where you're headed.

Let me share something with you? As a kid, maybe your parents gave you everything they never had. Maybe they tried to live through you, shaping your life, steering your choices, and molding your path. And maybe, even now, you still feel like you're trying to live up to someone else's idea of who you should be. That stops now. To be free from other people's expectations is finally letting your unique self shine.

For years, people have shared the story of a baby elephant born in captivity. When it was born, a rope was tied around its leg and pinned to the ground. The newborn elephant struggled and pulled, but it was too weak and small. Eventually, it gave up.

That same elephant grew up to become huge and powerful. But it remained tied to the same small stake, unaware that it could break free at any moment. This was because it had been taught to believe it couldn't.

You're just like the elephant. You're powerful beyond measure. But your past—the conditioning, fear, and limitations others have placed on you—has convinced you to stay small.

Like that baby elephant tied to a stake, you grow up thinking the rope still has power. You don't realize you could easily rip it out of the ground. That's what drifting does—it convinces you to believe in false limits.

The opposition—the voice of fear, doubt, and distraction—wants you to be passive and obedient. It wants you to drift.

It whispers lies: "Play it safe." "Don't make waves." "Who are you to rise up?" It doesn't want you to think for yourself. Because once you do, you become unstoppable. But I'm here to tell you something: That rope is fake. It was never stronger than you.

It's time to wake up. It's time to break free from the hypnotic trance of limitation. To stop sleepwalking through life while your potential rots in the corner. You were never meant to just survive—you were meant to lead, build, create, and elevate.

You regain your power whenever you choose courage over fear, discipline over distraction, or faith over doubt.

So ask yourself:

Who benefits from your silence?

Who profits when you forget who you are?

And then remind yourself: You're not here to drift.

You're here to dominate your path.

To outwit the fear.

To dismantle the lies.

To reclaim your destiny.

The chains were never real.

The gate was never locked.

The only thing you needed was the courage to pull.

Now's the time. It's time to remember who you are and become who you were born to be.

Bonus Principle: Play Chess, not Checkers

Most people in life are playing checkers – making quick moves, short jumps, and no real strategy. But life is like chess. It's about being patient, positioning yourself, and seeing the bigger picture, not just reacting to what's in front of you. Checkers is about making moves. Chess is about finding meaning.

You thought you knew the truth, but only saw what your ego wanted you to see, not what was really there. In chess, you get checkmated if you don't keep your ego in check.

That's how life works, too. Every piece has a purpose. The King doesn't move fast, but he moves wisely, one step at a time – because one wrong move is game over. The Queen is mighty, moving in all directions. She's not behind the King, she's beside him, holding the kingdom together. The Rooks move straight;

they're focused, driven, and have no distractions. The Bishops move diagonally; they're unorthodox thinkers who see the angles that no one else does. The Knights jump over obstacles, quiet but dangerous, moving differently. The Pawns are on the front lines, loyal, limited at first, but if they keep moving forward, they can become anything... except the King. And that's the beauty of growth.

In your life, you might be the King. You might be the Rook or the Knight in someone else's life. We all play different roles in different people's lives, which makes the whole thing work. Individually, each piece has limits, but together they're unstoppable. That's a kingdom. So, here's your choice: you can keep playing checkers – fast, reactive, emotional – or you can start playing chess strategically, intentionally, and aware. One is survival, the other is mastery.

Are you reacting like a checkers player or making moves like a chess master, building a lasting legacy?

Thought-Provoking Question

What old stake are you still attached to, and who would you be if you finally ripped it from the ground?

ABOUT THE AUTHOR

Frederick A. Martinez (Fred Martinez) is a 21st-century alchemist, combining the expertise of a high-performance coach, seasoned athlete, speaker, and engineer to empower people to turn their struggles into purpose and become their strongest selves, both physically, mentally, and spiritually.

With over 40 years of experience in a wide range of sports, including baseball, basketball, football, tennis, track and field, powerlifting, weightlifting, and bodybuilding, Frederick deeply understands what it's like to be the underdog. As a Division I track sprinter and later a Team USA Master's Olympic Weightlifter competing on international stages like the Pan American Games and World Cup, he's never let limitations hold him back. Instead, he's used them as motivation.

Despite being underestimated—considered too small, not fast enough, and not the smartest in the room—Frederick rose above the challenges. He didn't do it easily, but by choosing to outgrow every excuse and overcome every setback.

Frederick is a certified expert in Neuro-Linguistic Programming (NLP), high-performance coaching, and sports performance hypnosis. He's also a Six Sigma Green Belt and a USA Weightlifting Sports Performance Coach. However, his greatest strength is in mindset—helping people rewrite their story, take back their power, and uncover the truth that exists beneath their pain.

He's the author of The Path Is The Way To Self-Mastery, What The F.R.E.D.!: Mastering the Four Essential Traits for an Unstoppable Mindset, and Financial Game Plan for Your Dollars and Cents. Additionally, he's a co-author of the international bestseller 1% More: The Hidden Force to Creating Extraordinary Results in Life & Business.

Frederick's life proves one thing: you don't have to be the biggest, fastest, or most talented—you just need to unleash the alchemist within.

Connect with Frederick: www.FredMartinez.info
www.fredmartinezauthor.com
www.risehigheracademy.com

ACKNOWLEDGEMENTS

To my family, thank you for being my rock. To my mom, Ramona Martinez, and dad, Alejandro "Alex" Martinez II—your unconditional love, resilience, and quiet strength showed me what true love is all about. To my brothers, Alex Martinez III and Leroy Martinez, and sisters, Yvonne Diaz, Karen Martinez, and Sharon Martinez—thank you for being by my side, for believing in me even when I didn't believe in myself. Your presence has been a steady force in my life, and I'm deeply grateful for your support.

My childhood friends, you sparked the spirit of adventure and laughter that still guides me today. The memories we shared weren't just moments—they were milestones. Thanks for showing me that joy and brotherhood are just as vital as discipline and perseverance.

To the coaches, mentors, and teachers who pushed me, shaped me, and saw something in me before I did—thank you for being mirrors of truth and possibility. You didn't just teach me a skill—you gave me the value of grit, humility, and purpose.

To my teammates, past and present—thank you for pushing me, lifting me up, and being there through the highs and lows. You taught me the value of teamwork and what it means to compete with heart, not just muscles. We didn't just train together—we shared a common goal.

This book represents every lesson, every sacrifice, and every act of love that led me here. I didn't walk this path alone, and I'll always remember those who helped me get here.

With love and deep respect,

Frederick A. Martinez

If you enjoyed this book, please consider leaving us a REVIEW.

We are truly grateful for each review we receive,
which helps us expand our reach.
Thank you very much!

QR Code here

OTHER BOOKS By
Frederick A.Martinez

www.ingramcontent.com/pod-product-compliance
Lightning Source LLC
Chambersburg PA
CBHW071521120626
46550CB00006B/2305